TO WH‖‖‖‖D1234222‖‖‖‖
READS THIS BOOK:

GOD BLESS YOU!

FOR MORE COPIES

GO TO

WEST BOW
PRESS
(ONLINE)

Rebecca Ann-
717-272-0817

Broken
CHAINS

Breaking the Bonds of Satan

Rebecca Ann

WestBow
PRESS
A DIVISION OF THOMAS NELSON

WestBow Press books may be ordered through booksellers or by contacting:

WestBow Press
A Division of Thomas Nelson
1663 Liberty Drive
Bloomington, IN 47403
www.westbowpress.com
1-(866) 928-1240

Because of the dynamic nature of the Internet, any web addresses or
links contained in this book may have changed since publication and
may no longer be valid. The views expressed in this work are solely those
of the author and do not necessarily reflect the views of the publisher,
and the publisher hereby disclaims any responsibility for them.

Any people depicted in stock imagery provided by Thinkstock are models,
and such images are being used for illustrative purposes only.

Certain stock imagery © Thinkstock.

ISBN: 978-1-4497-1511-3 (sc)

Library of Congress Control Number: 2011930024

Printed in the United States of America

WestBow Press rev. date: 6/8/2011

Chapter 1
The Beginning

Satan binds people that aren't expecting him to strike. I was blinded by all my mistakes. I made decisions and choices that I don't want anyone else to have to experience. I thought I was an average person with nothing to worry about. I was born in a small town in Pennsylvania. Born into a dysfunctional family, my mother was sixteen and my father several years older than her when she gave birth to me. My parents only married due to the pregnancy, thus beginning a rough life.

My father worked as a gas station attendant most of his life. He was very seldom at home, suffering from an alcohol addiction. Every day he would work and come home to drink time away. Only coming home late, he left me at home with my mother. She had to watch me all day. I was the first of five. My brother was born only seventeen months after me. My mother was sick in and out of the hospital for unknown reasons at this time too.

About one year after my brother was born, my mother became sick and then had a miscarriage a year later. After five years of dealing with the tragedy, my sister was born. This occurred just as I was starting kindergarten. My mother was busy with the baby and had me walk a mile to the bus stop and back every school day. School was an escape for me even though I only had one friend. She was the only girl nice to me. All of the other children made fun of me and picked on me all of the time. They called me names and said hurtful things to me and it made it hard to go to school but I went to get away from my home life. I played by myself on the school playground until my brother began to come to school. When he came I had someone to play with on the school playground.

Even when the other children let me join in on their games, they made me feel terrible about myself. I continued to play with them out of desperation to have friends and be like the other children. I would do anything to play Farmer in the Dell, Four Square, or baseball. I never told my parents how the other children treated me at school. I didn't see the point in telling them because it wouldn't change anything. I always kept my feelings to myself for the same reason; telling someone wouldn't change anything and besides, I didn't have anyone to tell. I always sat by myself or with my brother on the school bus. I was always afraid of everyone and everything. As I continued my education I still yearned to be popular with the other children and have fun with everyone, which never happened.

My brother and I were always outside playing when we were at home. We played outside everyday, no matter what season it was. The love of being outside wasn't the only reason for being out; we didn't want to get in anyone's way. We always lived on farms in the country when we were young, making it easy to stay out of the way. My brother and I were always roaming the barns, fields, and pastures. I loved playing with my paper dolls outside when he wasn't around. I would make them houses out of old cardboard boxes. I loved to ride our scooter in the long dirt lane too. When my brother was outside with me we would play with his trucks in the dirt lane.

Chapter 2
The Pond

It was winter and the pond was frozen over. My brother wanted to go ice-skating. So young and naïve, we decided to go without my mother's supervision. At the time I was six and my brother five. We didn't think anything about the danger of our actions. What could have been better than ice-skating on such a nice winter day?

As we neared the pond our excitement grew. Packed in our snow attire, boots and all, we were set. At the pond my brother's excitement must have gotten the better of him because he rushed to the side of the pond. The next thing I knew, he had fallen in. I was unbelievably scared but I didn't want my brother to drown. I lay on my stomach, sprawled out on the ice, and submerged my arms in the frigid water to pull him out. Intending to pull him out, I was pulled in too.

In the water, the ice and pressure seemed as though it was sucking our legs upwards, wanting to keep us down forever. We struggled and tried extremely hard to get out from under the ice. Not making it any easier, we were fully dressed in winter attire, boots, jackets, mittens, etc. I felt as though I would never get out and see my family again. How we ever managed to escape the freezing water without drowning, I really don't know. Later in life I discovered it was by God's awesome grace that we were saved from the pond.

Chapter 3
Animals

We always had animals on the farm. I loved them all. We had a German Sheppard named Lady and she was my favorite. One day I noticed she hadn't been home at her normal time, so I figured she had been roaming through the woods. After time went by I knew she had gotten lost or something had happened. I was worried sick about her. I was heart broken.

A neighbor man came by and said he had found her. She had been caught by her right front paw in a fox trap. The neighbor returned her home by carrying her on horse back with her paw still in the trap. It was a wretched sight. My father removed the trap from her paw trying to help her. Lady's paw was barely hanging on. We didn't have the money to take her to the vet. We never had money for things like that. I cried for my dog constantly. She didn't deserve what had happened to her.

Lady would frequently lick her paw and I could tell it was hurting her. One day I was walking home from school down the dirt lane and I was thinking about Lady. Not very shocked, I found Lady's paw lying in the dirt. Her paw had fallen off. I picked it up and carried it the rest of the way home with me while tears streamed down my face. I showed it to my mother but she had no response. I couldn't believe she didn't care more. I went outside to find Lady who hobbled over to me with three legs and I cried as I hugged her tightly.

Lady learned to adapt to her three legs. She was always outside with my brother and I before her incident, and even after. Lady hobbled all over the place. One day Lady found a skunk roaming down the dirt lane. Of course my brother and I had to follow her and the skunk. My brother and I picked up sticks as we followed Lady and the skunk. We followed them down the dirt lane for what seemed like forever. All of a sudden Lady decided to get real close to the skunk and we all three got sprayed with the nasty skunk smell. Lady was frantically pawing her nose and whimpering. My brother and I ran back to the house and told mother what happened. Mother was not happy with us. Mother had to wash our clothes and hang them out on the wash lines for fresh air.

We had hens and chicks on our farm. They were adorable and my brother and I often followed the train of hen and chicks around. One day my brother decided to pick up a baby chick walking in the barnyard behind its mother. The hen turned as the baby chick chirped and started attacking my brother with her wings and claws. I screamed at my brother to let the baby chick go. My brother finally let the baby chick go and the hen stopped attacking him.

We also had ponies. My brother had a black pony named Midnight. My uncle would have a rope tied to the pony's bridal and we would ride Midnight around in circles in the field. I was riding Midnight and my uncle decided to remove the rope from the bridal. My uncle stated to me that I would be ok since I had been riding Midnight for a while. Without him holding the rope Midnight sensed I was scared and bucked me off. I went flying backwards off of Midnight and landed flat on my back on the ground. I cried and was still really scared. Up to this day I do not ride horses or ponies.

We also would receive colored peeps for Easter. The peeps were so cute. We would play with the peeps constantly and inevitably got attached. Eventually the peeps had grown to chickens. Our family killed and ate the chickens then. It was of course hard to do but it was quickly forgotten.

Chapter 4
Childhood

One day my brother and I were washing dishes after eating with the family. I was about seven now and my brother was around six. We thought it would be neat to put soapy dishwater on the kitchen floor and pretend it was an ice skating rink. So we put the water on the floor and started skating. Skating on the wet floor was fun until mother found us laughing on the floor and with our clothing drenched. My mother was not happy with us at all and sent us straight to bed for punishment.

I started to walk in my sleep around this age also. I would often wake up to find myself sleeping on the stair steps. I also woke up to find myself and all my bed linens at the opposite end of the bed I fell asleep at. I would then ask my mother why she placed me at the other end of the bed. She told me she did not move me. My mother realized I was sleepwalking.

I would also in my sleep, get out of bed and place a small rug over a wall light that had no cover on it. One night my mother had been woken up by the smell of something burning. She found the source to be the rug over the light. My mother asked me why I put the rug over the light and I said I did not know because I didn't remember putting the rug over the light at all. My mother knew I could not sleep with the light on, but we had to keep the light on because my sister, whom I shared a bedroom with, was afraid of the dark. My mother told me that was probably why I covered the light with the rug while I was sleepwalking. I eventually stopped sleepwalking, as I grew older.

My sister and I would fight when we were doing the dishes when she got older. I was washing the dishes and my sister was drying the dishes one day. We were fighting and I pushed her. Her dress caught on the side of the metal utensil drawer that was open. My sister's dress tore when it got caught on the drawer. When my mother found out I got in trouble for pushing and tearing her dress.

When my brother and I were around eight or nine we would still have to walk a country road to and from the bus stop for school. The three older neighbor boys were very mean to us. All three of them would chase my brother and I back the road until we would fall. It would make us both cry terribly. My tights would be torn and bloody at the knees.

One day these boys chased my brother and I back the road when all of a sudden they stopped. My brother and I then proceeded to walk home without thinking anything of it. Then all of a sudden one of the boys took a cupcake with icing and smeared it all over my brand new coat. I ran home crying and showed my mother. My mother showed my father when he had gotten home. My mother and father fought over confronting the parents of the boys and making the school aware. My mother and father never did confront the parents or make the school aware.

Chapter 5
The Separation

When my father was home all he and my mother did was fight. There was barely a time when they weren't fighting. They fought over money, his drinking, and his failure to be home more often than not. Two years later my youngest brother was born. We moved frequently from house to house for reasons unknown to me.

My mother decided she could no longer live with my father because of the constant disagreements between them. We moved and my father stayed behind in our home. This was really hard to deal with. I felt like my family had been broken. We always celebrated birthdays, Christmas, etc., with my aunts and uncles but it wasn't the same. We did not get a lot of presents for Christmas because the money wasn't there. We were accustomed to not having money by now though.

My one aunt and uncle were really close to my father. After my mother left my father things changed. My uncle would no longer come for the holidays because he didn't agree with my mother's decision to leave my father. This was also hard to deal with because it started to affect the entire family. Still I had no one to talk to and kept my feelings inside of me.

My mother complained everyday about my father; she would go on about how he was nothing but bad news. My maternal grandmother moved in with us. In the following days my mother found a job at a sewing factory. My grandmother had to babysit us while she was working. The farmhouse we moved into had no running water to the bathroom upstairs. We had to use an outhouse in the daytime and a chamber bucket during the night. It was one of my chores to empty the chamber bucket in the outhouse the next day. We also had no tub to take baths in. My mother had a large metal bathtub and we took baths in it when it was in front of the coal cook stove. All three of us older children had to use the same bath water. It wasn't a great condition to be living in.

My grandmother had a boyfriend who was an alcoholic and already married to another woman. He was at our house frequently. One day I was told to put a sweater on my baby brother who was only a couple months old. I was around ten or eleven years old at the time. My grandmother's boyfriend was watching me put the sweater on the baby and I bent his arm back instead of pulling the sleeve forward. Her boyfriend was mad at me for my small mistake. He yelled at me and frightened me. I started to run away from him. He grabbed me and turned me upside down and was swinging me by my feet. He continued to yell at me while I was swinging. My grandmother ran to rescue me and this caused an argument between them. I was so scared. When he let me go I ran outside and cried. After that incident I was scared. Whenever he was around, I stayed out of his way.

My mother let her sister move in with us also. She was a go-go girl at a local bar. My aunt had a boyfriend who also visited frequently. My aunt's boyfriend was using illegal drugs during this time. At such an early age, I seemed to be around the wrong people, without a choice. My mother took us to church one day with her youngest sister. This was my very first time in church.

When I was around thirteen, my aunt, who lived with us, had become pregnant, not with the boyfriend who was abusing illegal substances, but a new one. My mother went away and I was left to watch a pregnant adult, only being about ten years older. My mother also left me at home to watch the other children. My mother and grandmother would go away to a palm reader and their parenting responsibilities became mine.

One day while I was baby-sitting my younger brother who was about five years old. We were outside playing. My little brother was playing his trucks on the dirt floor of the garage. My little brother started crying. I went to the garage and saw a groundhog in the garage with my little brother. I did not know what to do. My instinct told me to help get my brother out of there. I called to my little brother to go to the other side of the garage and run out to me. When we told my mother what happened she scolded me and said I should have gone in the garage after my brother. I was afraid to go in the garage because I was always told not to corner a groundhog because they will attack you if they are cornered, so I thought it was safer for my little brother to come out to me instead of me going in after him.

My sister and I were always fighting. We shared a bedroom. Her side was always messy and my side was always clean. Her messiness drove me crazy, to the point where I took a piece of chalk and drew a line on the rug separating her side from my side. My sister was my dad's pick. I was no ones pick. Later in life I discovered how terrible it is to a child to be the child no one picks and how that affects them emotionally. That child feels unloved, unwanted and not good enough. That child also feels jealousy towards the child who is the pick as I felt towards my sister and had to deal with later in life.

Chapter 6
Rebellion

Later my mother switched sewing jobs. At this job my mother met a woman who was a Jehovah's Witness. She inspired my mother to start studying the Bible. My mother also started attending their meetings. She took all four of us children with her to these meetings. She met a man several years her junior at these meetings. My mother joined the Jehovah's Witnesses. My mother was later baptized as a Jehovah's Witness. I was never baptized though.

During this time my maternal great-grandmother became sick. I was fourteen and any time I was not at school, I was there to look after her. My great-grandmother became so sick I could not tend to her by myself anymore. My mother, grandmother, and us four children moved from a large house, into my great-grandmother's small home.

My mother announced when she joined the Jehovah's Witness's we would no longer celebrate holidays, birthdays, etc. This was hard to deal with. One day we are celebrating holidays and the next we are not celebrating the holidays. It was also hard because other children in school would come back to school after vacation and ask you what you got for Christmas. I would make stuff up because I did not want to be made fun of because I got nothing for Christmas. I started to be rebellious. I did not see eye-to-eye with my mother. I was glad only for one reason. I was able to quit band and chorus due to the religion. When I was in the band and chorus, the band would participate in holiday parades; the chorus would have Christmas programs. The parades and programs were not allowed by the religion. My mother made me join band in the fifth grade. I certainly did not want to join. I played the clarinet to please my mother.

Shortly there after joining the Jehovah's Witness's my mother announced she and her boyfriend were getting married. This man, who was going to marry my mother, was only a few years older than I. I was fifteen at the time and I hated him more than anything. He talked down to my mother and us. He was very controlling.

One day I had written to a friend about my feelings about the marriage and the religion. My letter was on the table to be mailed. My mother and her fiancé opened my letter and read it. They confronted me about my feelings. They were very upset with me. They took me to the back bedroom for a belt whipping. Her fiancé told me to bend over the bed with my clothes on so he could use the belt on me. I was mad and scared. My mother was by his side the entire time. I bent over and when he raised his hand with the belt, I pushed past my mother and ran out of the house and hid behind a large tree in the woods, behind the house. I could hear them calling me, but I was scared and wouldn't answer them. I finally answered them and told them I was calling Children and Youth. They didn't touch me after that.

I met this cute boy at the Kingdom Hall, where we attended meetings. I thought he was so cute and cool. He helped me to get to a phone booth to call Children and Youth. I was told nothing could be done because they did not touch me. Children and Youth also told me that I was too old, that people wanted younger children. Children and Youth called my mother and told her I called them. As soon as I got home my mother and her fiancé yelled at me.

On a later date I was talking to my girlfriend, from the Kingdom Hall, on the phone. Ironically, the guy I liked was a friend with her brother. When we were talking she asked me if I wanted to talk with this guy. Of course I said yes. I was talking to him on the phone when my mother, listening to me talking, asked me whom I was talking to. I was scared, but I told her it was my boyfriend. She grabbed the phone from me and slammed it down and told me I am not allowed to talk to boys on the phone. I went to my room and cried.

I could not talk to boys, celebrate holidays, wear short skirts as I did before, wear make-up, and associate with kids from school. This religion was separating me from anything outside its approval. I was only allowed to associate with children of the same religion. I was forced to go to the Kingdom Hall, give talks, and go out door to door. I hated it. I became even more rebellious.

I would wear a knee length skirt in the house in the morning before I would go to school. On the way to the bus stop I would lay my books down and roll my skirt up at the waste to make it shorter. On the way home from school I would lay my books down again and unroll my skirt to make it knee length again. I started wearing make-up. My mother would not buy it for me so my boyfriend bought my make-up. I associated with the kids at school, but not outside of school. I also continued to Pledge Allegiance in school, which I was told I had to stop because it was against the religion.

One day in the ninth grade at my new school we had to do a paper for English class about our home life. When my teacher returned my paper she stated to me, "Your life can not be all that dark". I could not believe a teacher would say something like that to a student. Needless to say I withdrew from that teacher and believed in my mind that all teachers felt the same way about me.

My great-grandmother passed away and my mother remarried. Her new husband told my grandmother she could no longer live with us after so many years of living with us. We moved again into a bigger house. This time the house was in the city, which meant that I had to change to the city schools. Changing schools as a teenager was hard. I also had to deal with my grandmother not living with us after so many years. My grandmother was like a second mother, who was very bossy. We children would call our grandmother Sergeant Pepper amongst ourselves. We also were not allowed to watch a lot of television shows due to the religion enforced constantly.

My mother did not like the boy I chose as my boyfriend. She was always making negative statements about him to me. I couldn't do anything to stand up for him then. I started sneaking around with him because I knew she didn't approve of him. My boy friend was three years older than me. I was fifteen almost sixteen. I had asked my mother a question regarding sex. My mother's response was that I was too young to be thinking about boys. I never asked my mother about sex again.

My stepfather left a male friend of his live with us also. This friend had a crush on me. I couldn't stand him. I had to pull a red wagon with baskets of dirty wash to the Laundromat every week. I had to wash, dry, and fold the wash, most of which was not mine. I had to iron the wash. I also had to iron the friends dress shirts, which were many. I hated it. I started not ironing the friend's shirts and just hanging them in the back of his other shirts. The friend told my stepfather and I got in trouble for not ironing all his shirts. I yelled at my stepfather. I said, "I am not his wife. He can iron his own shirts."

I started swearing and sneaking around with my boyfriend even more. My boyfriend could drive and had a car. One time I did the laundry and took it home. I went in the front door and sneaked out the back. My mother and stepfather came looking for me at my boyfriend's house. I hid in the closet so they could not find me. My boyfriend took me home later that afternoon. I was in trouble with my mother and stepfather. Of course I lied to them about where I was and what I was doing.

My mother found a job at a chocolate factory in a nearby town. This is when I had more chores to attend to, cooking, cleaning, and more. My mother then became pregnant with my half-sister, her fifth child. My mother had problems with this pregnancy. Her job was also swing shift and interfered with the religion and meetings. My stepfather made my mother quit her job. We were poor again. He worked at a ball factory making minimum wage. We had to move again because they could no longer afford the house payments after my mother had to quit the chocolate factory.

We, all six of us, moved into his parents run down shack, in another part of the city. The shack was even smaller than my great-grandmother's house and the bathroom had a dirt floor. My sister and I slept in the only bedroom upstairs. My two brothers slept in the kitchen on bunk beds. My mother and her husband slept in the other bedroom downstairs.

I started skipping school. One time I skipped school for two weeks straight. My boyfriend had graduated from high school and did not have a job as of yet. So I skipped for two weeks and hung out with him running around to the park and shopping plaza. My boyfriend took me to his doctor so I could have a doctor's note to return to school. I faked having a sore throat. The doctor gave me a note for school for the past two weeks. I thought I was so cool. I would get up in the morning and get ready for school and leave like I was going to school. I would meet my boyfriend down the street. He would pick me up and then when school time would be over he would drop me off and I would go home like I was in school for the day.

I did this until the Friday of the second week when I walked in the door and my mother asked me how school was and where was my homework. I told her I did not have any homework and school was fine. I asked her why she was asking me because she never asked me such things before. She then proceeded to tell me the school called her and asked her when I was returning to school from my illness. The school and my mother then figured out I was skipping school. I had a lot of consequences. I was not allowed to go to my girlfriend's house that was of the same religion. I also had school detention for the rest of the school year, which was about three weeks.

I tried smoking cigarettes and pot. I never inhaled, but it was the "cool" thing to do. I started having sex with my boyfriend, who taught me all about sex. I was now seventeen. I was not allowed to get a job because it would interfere with the religion, and the meetings. I was not allowed to get my drivers license either.

I hated my stepfather more than ever. He was meaner to us. I could not listen to certain music anymore. My boyfriend would buy me forty-five records. My stepfather who did not like my forty-five records took them from my room when I was not home and hid them in his room. I do not remember how long it was until I got them back. I would yell at my stepfather that he was not my father and that he could not tell me what to do.

Chapter 7
Dad

After that I went to live with my real father, who was single. My father found an apartment in the country for him and I. I had to change to country schools again. I began losing count on how many times I moved and enrolled in schools. I got a job after school in a chicken factory with a girlfriend I met at this school. I often walked by myself to and from work, unless my friend's boyfriend would pick me up.

I broke up with my boyfriend, and I found another boyfriend. I then broke up with him because he was too nice to me and would insist on not having sex with me. I did not know how to deal with people being nice to me. I thought there was something wrong with me. I also did not know how to deal with a boy not wanting to have sex with me. I would question myself, am I ugly, am I too fat, what is wrong with me that this boy would not have sex with me? Later in life and after counseling I realized how dysfunctional I was in my life and my thinking. I was looking for someone to love me in the wrong way and places. I later though realized that the boyfriend that was nice to me would have made a good husband.

I started hanging at the bars with my dad and his friend. They would put shots in my sodas when we went to the Legion. One time the bartender came over and tested my soda. The soda had no shots in it at the time. I was given a free soda.

I almost got myself raped by two men from the bar I frequented with my dad. A boy form school, who was friends with my girlfriend and I, was at the bar also with his cousin. This boy came over and asked me if I would go drinking somewhere else with the guys. I said, "Sure, why not?" I now had the attention of two guys. I never gave a thought as to what could happen to me with two guys. We picked up a bottle of Vodka and started drinking. I do not know where we drove to, but it was dark outside and the driver parked the car. He then proceeded to kiss me. I got scared and started saying, "Take me home. Take me home." He wanted to keep kissing me. I pushed he away and yelled, "Take me home! Take me home!" He became angry but they took me home. I was so scared on the way home.

When I got inside the apartment that was in the country, I realized while this guy was kissing me the other guy was going through my purse and took all my money out of my wallet. I sat on the floor by myself because my dad was still at the bar and cried and cried. I realized what I had gotten myself into and how fortunate I was that I was not raped. I did not tell anybody because there was no adult I had to talk with. God was with me that night and saved me from my destructive behavior. Today I get down on bended knees and thank God for saving me that night.

I often walked home from the bar by myself. It was a long walk down a dark country road. I was walking home one night when a car drove past me and the man did a double take. I had long blond hair, blue eyes and was skinny. I was scared. I ran and hid behind a big tree because I had a feeling he was coming back. He did come back. I stayed behind the tree and watched him turn around in the dirt cul-de-sac and look for me. He went past the tree I was behind and when he was leaving I ran to the apartment as fast as I could. This man came back again and looked for me. I was peaking out the window. I locked the door and kept the lights off. I was scared. I was home alone because dad was at the bar. Fortunately nothing happened that night.

Chapter 8
The Wedding

A couple of weeks later I started dating a married man, whose wife left him because of me. Later in life I learned that this married man was an alcoholic. I lived with my father a couple of months when he told me he could no longer afford to keep me. I did not know what to do. I did not want to go home with my mother, so I called my aunt. She said I could live with her. Her two daughters were small children. I knew she wanted me as a built in baby sitter. I was not going to live there as a built in baby sitter.

I had to beg my stepfather to allow me to come back home. I had to agree to his rules and orders. I had nowhere else to live, so I moved back home with my mother, stepfather and my three siblings. Shortly there after, my mother gave birth to my half-sister. My sister and I were responsible for taking care of our baby sister. She slept in the living room in a bassinet.

By moving back in with my mom, I had to change back to the city schools. I started falling behind in school because the country school was too far behind the city schools for me to catch up. I had to change courses in school in order to pass my junior year so I could make it into my senior year.

During the summer months I went back to my first boyfriend. I discovered in November of my senior year that I was pregnant. I was afraid to tell my mother I was pregnant. I never asked my mother for birth control pills because her religious belief was to not use artificial birth control. My mother's belief was to use the natural rhythm method. When I finally told my mother she was upset with me and stated I had to get married because that's the biblical thing to do in this situation.

My boyfriend and I got married in February of my senior year. My mother would not help me with planning my wedding. She did tell me I could not wear white for a wedding dress because I was no longer a virgin. My mother and stepfather did not attend my wedding because I was pregnant. My aunt, who had the two little girls, helped me with my wedding. I got married at my aunt's house. I wore a maroon velvet gown. A Justice of the Peace married us and my father gave me away. My aunt, grandmother, two cousins and his parents were the only witnesses to the wedding. After the wedding we went to a local diner's banquet room for the reception with about one hundred people attending. My aunt paid for the reception and cake for us. My mother and stepfather didn't help. They did not attend the reception either. After the reception my husband and I stopped at my mother's house so she could see me in my gown.

We found an apartment in the country and moved in prior to the wedding. I turned eighteen in April and I went to school pregnant in my senior year. I graduated from high school in the end of May. June fifteenth I gave birth to a baby girl. She had a head full of dark hair. My new husband was not very helpful with the baby. She cried a lot. He worked at a steel foundry and I was a housewife. I did not have a baby shower. My friend from high school brought me a baby gift. She stopped being my friend and

I did not know why until after I divorced my husband. I ran into her and she made me aware that my husband was propositioning her.

One day my husband was fighting with me and I threw a baby bottle at him and hit him in the head with the bottle. I ran as fast as I could upstairs to the bedroom with the baby and locked the door. He banged on the door. I was scared and would not open the door until sometime later when he calmed down.

A few weeks late he taught me how to drive a car. I didn't need much practice. Soon afterwards, I proceeded to obtain my drivers license.

Chapter 9
My Sister

Eighteen months later I gave birth to another baby girl. My husband wanted a son and still was not very helpful. During this time, my sister became ill. The doctors said she had mono. My sister was hospitalized. She was later transferred to a better-equipped hospital. I had my two daughters at this time. My stepfather never went to the hospital to see my sister. He never took my mother to see my sister. My grandmother took my mother to see my sister. My sister passed away at the age of sixteen, due to a weak immune system from the mono. I was sad and happy for my sister. I was sad because I would miss her, even though we fought all the time. I was glad because she was in a better place and did not have to be around all the hurt we had to deal with because of the dysfunctional family and the religion.

My mother never visited my sister's gravesite after the initial burial. My sister had this tiny name plaque for years. Later when my father passed away, he was buried beside my sister. I purchased a nice name plaque for the both of them to share.

I took over my sister's job after she passed way. I was working in the laundry at the county nursing home. My sister was allowed to have a job because my grandmother also worked there. She took my sister to and from work with her. Her job also did not interfere with the Witness meetings, because it was dayshift hours.

I had to quit my job not long after I started. I had to quit due to my husband calling me at work all the time. He was laid off at the time and was watching the girls while I worked. He was tired of watching the girls. He would call my work and tell them one of my daughters was sick when she was not. He couldn't handle watching them so I had to quit even though I didn't want to.

Two years later I gave birth to a son. I was in labor for twenty-seven hours. My water ruptured early without contractions. I could no longer deal with the dry birth. I asked my doctor to do a c-section. He told me I was too far into labor. My son was a large baby for my stature. Several blood vessels in my face ruptured. I had to stay a few extra days in the hospital.

I was taught the Witnesses do not believe in birth control. So I did not use any. I later started using birth control. I was not baptized as a Jehovah Witness, but I had years of rules drilled into my head. If I did something I should not have, I heard my mother's voice in the back of my head say Jehovah does not approve of this. I could not talk to my mother as a daughter and mother. She would always respond with Jehovah this and Jehovah that.

Chapter 10
My Fault

My husband and I moved three times. His parents bought a house, and they gave us their old shack. The shack had holes in the roof. One day we were away and it rained in all over the girls' dresser. I cried. I said that was all I could take. I couldn't take anymore. I had enough. I told my husband I was tearing the old house down and using the lot to build a new house. I did all the research and work to find a contractor to build our home. My husband did nothing but tag along. We were starting to fight a lot.

I eventually found a contractor. We tore down the old shack ourselves. We had to store our furniture in the basement of my husband's cousin's house. The children and I went to live with my dad in his three-bedroom trailer. The house building was only to take three months. It turned out to take six months. It was during this time that it had snowed. There was a thick layer of ice on top of the ground. The next time it rained, the rain could not seep into the ground due to the layer of ice. At my husband's cousin's house there was flooding in the basement where our furniture was stored. We lost everything we had stored there. The insurance company would not cover our losses because the furniture was not at the address on the policy. I felt like I could not get ahead for anything. I cried because we did not have the money to purchase new furniture. I cried even more because my husband told me to stop my balling and deal with it.

My husband stayed with his parents. He visited us when he was off work. We started making love one time he was visiting us and he did not want me to get out of bed for birth control. Two months later I was pregnant. I was getting depressed, tired of everything. I did not want another child. I already had four children (including my husband), lost all our furniture, and the house was still not completed. Fortunately I managed to salvage some pictures from the flooded basement.

We moved into the new house in the summer. There was a playground near by and I took the children there almost every evening to play on the swings, sandbox, etc. The children were happy. They could now have a swing set that my father bought them at the new house. The house was a square two-story house. It had three bedrooms and bath upstairs. Downstairs there was a large kitchen and living room. It was the best home I ever lived in my whole life. Up to that point I cooked, cleaned, did the laundry and did the outside work. I mowed the lawn and everything else.

We were fighting more because he was doing nothing. My husband was swearing at me more and calling me names. He started skipping work more frequently. I was still depressed and I was losing weight in my pregnancy, the doctor told me if I did not gain weight by my sixth month he was going to hospitalize me. I gained a few pounds by my sixth month. I gave birth to a baby girl in December. I was so depressed. The doctor told me my child was born with a birth defect. She had a severe right clubfoot. I cried on the first night I got to hold her and feed her.

While I was holding her, she did not cry and she started turning blue. I rang the bell for the nurse. The nurse took my baby. I was scared and crying. The nurse came back in a little bit later and stated the baby had a mucus plug and could not get it up. They proceeded to suction her and she was fine after that. I felt scared when I feed her for a while there after because I did not know if she would get another mucus plug. I felt so guilty for her birth defect because I lost weight in the beginning of my pregnancy. It took me a long time to get rid of feeling guilty for her birth defect.

My father had a heart attack and came to live with us in September before I had my fourth child. I was twenty-three and a half and I had four children. My husband did not help at all. My youngest daughter had her first cast put on her right clubfoot when she was two days old in the hospital. Every two weeks she had to go to the doctor for a new cast. I had to soak and take off the old cast. She had her first foot surgery when she was six months old. She had several foot surgeries after that. She also had special shoes on a bar for a period of time after she was finished with the casts. She then went to special shoes, which were different sizes due to her feet being two different sizes. The right foot eventually needed a thicker sole on the shoe.

My husband was becoming more verbally abusive to my children and I. He was starting to skip work more frequently. He would come home shortly after he left for work, and state there was something wrong with the car. My father checked the car because my father was a mechanic. My father stated a car would steam if someone takes a screwdriver and punctures a hole in the water hose. When I confronted my husband he denied it, swore and yelled at me.

Another time he came home and stated a bird flew into the windshield of the van and cracked the windshield. My husband had a laceration on his forehead. He stated the laceration happened when the bird flew into the window of the van. Later it turned out to be a self-inflected wound. He called off work again. My father stated after he checked out the van, that the windshield was broken from the inside. When I confronted my husband, how a bird cracked the windshield from the inside of the van, he became furious. He yelled and called me names, and denied it.

My husband became sick, so he said. He had the shakes and was sweaty. When we were at MH/MR for help, they asked him if he was doing drugs because this is the behavior of someone in withdrawal from drugs or alcohol. Of course he denied it. Things got worse. My husband went to a psych hospital so he would not have to work. He was there for two weeks. He later tried to go back a second time but they refused to let him come back because he did not participate in the classes. When he was there he just lounged around on the benches outside.

My husband started acting weirder and was sleeping in our basement. His parents came up and jumped all over me and were saying that he was dying. I could not reason with them that he was not dying. He told his parents that he did not eat or drink for two weeks. He was not dying; he just did not want to work. All he did was smoke cigarettes and drink coke soda, watch television and yell and swear at us. He would yell "shut that kid the **** up or I'll shut it up". I would run and make the child stop crying so he would not hurt him or her.

My son started getting sick when he was two and a half. He became pale and tired. He had blood blisters on his tongue and he had Petechiae on his arms. I called the doctor. My son was diagnosed with ALL, Acute Lymphocytic Leukemia, which is frequently called cancer of the blood. My son was hospitalized for two weeks. I was scared he would die. I had no clue what I was doing. I had no medical knowledge and I also had no one to talk to. I later became friends with a Mennonite woman whose son also had Leukemia. I could talk a little bit with her. She left one week after my son's admission to the hospital due to her son's passing away.

I stayed with my son day and night for the two weeks he was hospitalized. I only went home to take a shower and put on clean clothes. The first bone marrow test they did on him he screamed and screamed and the doctor standing beside me took me out of the room before I passed out. I do not know where my husband was at this time. The doctors wanted to give him blood transfusions. I refused because Jehovah Witness's do not get blood transfusions. The hospital staff went to the judge and took temporary custody of my son. I was scared. My husband was angry and yelled, "Why did you do that? Now he will die."

I was fighting with myself because I was taught not to take blood transfusions but I also did not want my son to die because I refused him a blood transfusion. I do not remember who came and talked to me but I did not want my son to die because I did not give him a blood transfusion. I then gave my permission for him to have blood transfusions. The court then gave custody back to me and had a staff member come and talk to me after my son was discharged from the hospital. My son had bone marrow tests, IV's, blood work etc. frequently during his hospital stay. He also started chemotherapy in the hospital.

My father in law kept my youngest daughter. While my son was hospitalized my husband's cousin kept my older two daughters and sent them to school. While my son was hospitalized my mother visited my son one time and her sole purpose was to see if I let him have a blood transfusion. I know she was upset with me because I let them give him several blood transfusions. I could not be the cause of his death. My mother was no support for me. My son had eight units of blood. His blood was sixty-eight percent full of Leukemia cells when we arrived at the hospital. My son started chemo and went right into remission.

I had to take him every week for treatments at a hospital about half hour away. I also had to give him many medications at home. I marked what to give and when to give it on the calendar so I would not make a mistake. This was very stressful in addition to all my other duties. I also had to take him to the local pediatrician for an injection every week. We would have to wait for half an hour after the injection to make sure he had no reaction. I also had to take my daughter for her new casts. My husband did nothing to help.

Later on in chemotherapy, I had to take my son to the hospital for two weeks straight for radiation to the brain. I would always take a basin with me because he frequently vomited on the way home. My son lost all his hair from the radiation treatments. I frequently would have to take my son to the hospital several times a week for chemotherapy due to his blood veins being weak and blowing. The doctors and nurses would only stick him with needles two or three times and would tell me I had to bring him back another day so they could try again.

When my son came home from the hospital, he was crying and my husband picked him up with fists on the front of his shirt and put him up against the wall to punch him. I screamed at my husband to stop and let him go. I ran over and grabbed my son, who was crying hysterically. My father was sitting at the table and witnessed the incident.

Chapter 11
Sick of Everything

My husband did not sleep in bed with me for years after we got rid of his twin bed he had at home; he slept on the living room floor or couch. He would always fall asleep with cigarettes in his mouth. I had burn holes in the furniture. I was afraid to sleep. I was afraid that he would start the house on fire or harm the children or me during the night.

My husband became angry with my oldest daughter who was around six or seven years old and had a hard time with schoolwork. She was sitting at the table with schoolwork and he started kicking the bench she was sitting on. She started crying. I protected her from him by removing her from the bench and helping her with her schoolwork. I could not take any more as I became more depressed.

My husband would take money I had hidden under the mattress for diaper service. We did not have a checking account at this time. I would pay the bills I could. I kept money under the mattress to pay for my diaper service for the babies. I was angry with him. My husband also stole money from my father who lived with us. One day my father became ill and needed to go to the hospital. My husband took my father to the hospital. I could not take my father because I was taking care of our sick children. When they admitted my father to the hospital he gave my husband his wallet. My husband gave me the wallet when he returned from the hospital I did not look inside the wallet because it was not mine. I put the wallet in my father's room. When my father was discharged from the hospital he went to his room and checked his wallet. My father knew how my husband was even though I did not want to believe he would do such a thing. My father had one hundred dollars in his wallet that was now gone. When I confronted my husband he became angry and denied it.

We had a small Toyota with a hole in the floorboard. I put a piece of plywood over the hole to protect the children from falling through. We could not afford another car. I received WIC for my children. My husband went to the food bank several times due to the fact we had no money because he did not want to work. They told him he could no longer come back for help without a review of our finances. My husband had a good paying job at the steel foundry but because he skipped work all the time we were poor.

I went to a lawyer to see what I needed to do for a divorce. This was hard because Jehovah Witness's do not divorce, which was drilled into my head. I was fighting with myself over divorcing my husband. I could not take anymore though. I was afraid to tell my husband I went to the lawyer, but I eventually did. He promised me things would be different.

He did not change; he still did nothing and continued with his abusive behavior towards the children and I. He continued to accuse me of cheating on him all the time. He accused me of cheating with the diaper service man because he would say good morning to me and ask me how I was. He also accused me of cheating on him with the mailman because the mailman would say hello to me. My husband would then wait for the mail so I could not get it. I never cheated on my husband the nine and a half years I stayed with him. He was the one who cheated on me from almost day one but I didn't find out until I divorced him.

My husband said he would go to counseling with me. We went to counseling at the Psych hospital where he was previously an outpatient. One time during a counseling session my husband became angry with me and picked up the crayons our daughter was playing with and threw them at me. The counselor told him there would be no violence in this room. Things became worse between us.

When I was outside in the yard talking to my grandmother, my husband opened the upstairs window and threw a bucket of cold water on me. He laughed at me and thought he was funny. He would also wait until I was in the shower and he would throw cold water on me. He would then stand there and laugh at me. I did not lock the door in case the children needed me and they could come in the bathroom to me.

One day I went with his mother to yard sales. I left the youngest two children with him (my son and daughter). When I returned home my children were at the neighbor's house. I went over for my children. The neighbor lady stated she heard him swearing and yelling at the youngest daughter who was about fifteen-months old. She could not walk because of her feet being hooked on a brace bar. My daughter had a red right eye. My son was ok. When I confronted my husband, he stated the neighbor was not telling the truth, that our daughter fell down the steps and brushed burned her eye. Later her eye turned black and blue. I accused him of punching her in the eye. Of course he denied it. I was afraid to let my two youngest children home alone with him any more. I took my two youngest children with me where ever I went after that incident.

Another time I came home with my two youngest children and my second oldest daughter came running out the front door of the house crying and said, "Daddy fell down the steps." When I went in the house my husband was on his back at the bottom of the steps with my planter on top of him with no dirt on the floor. I called him on the incident. I questioned how he could fall down the steps, hit the half moon table and knock the planter on top of him without getting dirt on the floor. He gave me some off the wall answer, which I knew was not true. Again he reported off of work due to hurting his back when he supposedly fell.

From that time on I was afraid to leave any of my four children with him. I took four children grocery shopping with me. Taking four small children to the grocery store, pushing a shopping cart, getting your groceries, and keeping your children well behaved all at one time was nearly impossible. Well I did it all the time. It was very overwhelming. I took the four children with me to the dentist, clothing store, etc. I also took them with me to my son's chemo appointments. The only time I did not take them with me was when his mother watched them, which was seldom because my appointments were during the day when she worked. My mother never babysat my children. My depression worsened.

Chapter 12
That's It. I'm Done.

I stopped going with my husband to counseling because it wasn't helping. One day on the way home from the hospital from my son's chemo treatment, I was so depressed. I could not see any way out of my situation. I was going to drive off the road into a water filled quarry. I had all four children with me. I was thinking if I took all my children with me then no one would have to worry about them or me. As I was driving closer there was a voice in my head that said, "What happens if you die and your children live?" I do not know why I did not drive into the quarry that day. But when that voice in the back of my head spoke I knew there was no way I was leaving my children behind. I did not drive into the quarry. As I drove the rest of the way home I hated myself for thinking like that. I later in life realized that it was God saving my children and me from my destructive thoughts and behavior. God later showed me a way out of the cycles I was caught up in.

Not long after that day, I called a woman's shelter in a nearby county to see if my children and I could come there. The lady put me on hold for a few minutes to let me think about my request, when she returned to the phone I stated I still wanted to go to the shelter. After my husband left for work on the night shift, I took my four children and drove to the woman's shelter. I left all our belongings at the house when I left except for a few clothes and toys.

My husband thought I would never leave him. He always told me I was stupid, that I didn't have a job, and who would want a woman with four children: one with a birth defect, and one with cancer. I just knew I wanted out of the marriage and away from him. God gave me the strength and courage to leave this abusive relationship. I thank God for this strength and courage. That was the first good thing I did for my children and myself. My husband tried to contact me at the shelter, but he could not. I was safe there.

My children and I stayed at the shelter for one month. The shelter had a school program for the children. I tried to get my lawyer to get my husband out of the house. I wanted to move back in with my children. My husband refused to move out and they could not make him leave. He refused to give the children their clothing. I then had to obtain a constable to go with me and retrieve their clothing. I had to hire an attorney to go to court to split the furniture and belongings. When I went to pick up my share of the furniture, on the coffee table he was forced to give me, he took a knife and vandalized the top of it. The washer I was given had cigarette butts shoved down the hoses, clogging them.

I went to live with my mother and the family that was still home. I had to change my children's school. My husband would sneak around the house where my mother lived and check up on me. I finally filed for a divorce. At first my husband contested the divorce and said he would not sign the papers for three years, which I would then legally be divorced. One year later he signed the papers, because he found a girlfriend whom he wanted to marry. At last I was no longer married to him after nine and a half years of abuse.

As I said before that was the first best thing I did for my children and myself. I filed for child support and spousal support also. My ex husband had to pay child support but not spouse support. I lived with my mother for one year. I tried very hard and frequently during that year to get my house back. I did not get the house back. My ex husband did not make the mortgage payments. He trashed the house by letting dogs live and mess in the house and not cleaning the house. We were going to receive a sheriff sale on the house, but then a realtor saved us by purchasing the house at the last minute. We sold the home for enough money to pay the remainder of the mortgage. There was no money left to pay the lean on the house. The company had to absorb the loss, which in turn gave us bad credit.

My ex husband filed for full custody of our children. I had to hire an attorney and go to court to fight for my children. I won full custody of our children, my ex husband had visitation rights. He would come for the children when he felt like it. The children would wait for him and he would not show up. I would be afraid when my children went with him for visitation. I was scared for their safety while the children were with him. My ex husband had stopped paying child support and he became in the arrears. I could not work at the time due to all the doctor appointments for the children. I had to apply for public assistance.

Chapter 13
Moving On

When I was at the shelter I met a woman friend. She later introduced me to a man. This man and I waited until I was divorced to start dating. I found an apartment for my children and I. We moved into the apartment. I had to change schools again for my children. My youngest daughter at this time had to have hip surgery at the age of four. The hospital was forty-five minutes to one hour away. I would drop off my other three children at the babysitters who I found through a church organization. I did not have to pay for the babysitting due to my low income. I traveled over to the hospital every morning and came back home in the late afternoon. The doctors discovered she had a dislocated hip from birth and it was missed. Upon her physical exam they found her right leg was shorter then her left leg. She needed a higher sole on her right shoe and walked with more of a limp as she grew older which prompted the orthopedic doctor to take x-rays and discovered the dislocated right hip. She was in the hospital for four weeks. She had to be in skeletal traction for three weeks before the surgery to slowly pull the ball of the femur down to put in place after the hip surgery.

The doctor said he could not just put the femur ball in the hip socket because it was dislocated for several years and the sudden pressure from placement would cause the ball to die. When my daughter was discharged from the hospital she had a hip cast in place. She could not walk with this cast on. I would have to carry her everywhere she wanted to go. She would cry because she could not go outside and play with her siblings. I would have to put plastic wrap around the cast legs when she needed to use the toilet so the urine would not absorb into the cast. It was quite a chore.

I dated this man for one year, when he asked me to move back into my former house that was purchased and put up for rent. I did move into the house with him and my children. The realtor who purchased the house wanted to sell it to us. We tried to buy the house, but this man had bad credit. The realtor put the house up for sale. We then had to rent another house.

Things were fine at first. This man could not read. I felt sorry for him and I thought I could fix him. I also desperately wanted someone to love me. He started to become controlling and watching everything I did. My ex husband reported us to children and youth and stated that my boyfriend sexually abused my girls. I had to take my girls to the children and youth office. The woman there took my girls into another room and talked to them. When she returned with the girls she stated there is no reason for this report and closed the case. He also reported me to children and youth for my daughters standing out in the cold winter with dresses and no socks on their feet. The caseworker from children and youth came to the house and spoke with me. I told her I did not know what she was talking about. She asked me a few question and closed the case.

My youngest daughter who could now walk had to start school. Public assistance told me I needed to get a job because my youngest child was going to school. I had no job training. Public assistance sent me to some classes to see what training I qualified for. I qualified for the nursing program, so I enrolled in the nursing program. The man I was living with did not want me to go to school, because he did not want me to be better than him.

My ex-husband called me on the phone when he found out I was going to nursing school and said, "You will never pass the course. You're too stupid." That statement made me angry and made me more determined to do well in school. My mother also expressed her feelings regarding me not going to nursing school and me having to deal with blood. I proceeded to go to nursing school without support from my family. I had to leave my four children alone at home while I had to go to school. I could not afford a babysitter. My oldest daughter was thirteen and had completed a babysitter's course at a nearby hospital. I felt terrible leaving the children alone but I had no choice. Nursing school started in mid July. It was better when the children went back to school. Nursing school was hard. The school crammed two years of training into one year. I stayed up until two o'clock in the morning sometimes. I liked the nursing course. I started seeing the man I was living with differently. I was feeling controlled. I finished nursing school, and I took my state boards. After nursing school I found a part time job at the county nursing home as a GPN. I passed my state boards and became an LPN. To this day I am still an LPN at the same nursing home. As soon as I got my job as a GPN I moved to an apartment with my four children.

One day this man I used to be living with came to my apartment to take back the car I had. The car was in his name but I made the payments. I could not get a loan because my ex-husband ruined our credit. This man was fighting with me at the car. We were screaming at each other, back and forth. My daughter hit him with a bag of corn on the cob as we were unloading groceries. I was not living with this man for several months and he had no right to take the car back. I called the police. An officer came to my apartment and told me there was nothing I could do because the car was in his name. I learned a lesson from everything that had happened that day.

I stayed friends with my brother's ex-wife. She introduced me to her brother who was also divorced. He and I started talking for a while and got to know each other. After a while, we started dating. When my ex boyfriend took the car from me, my new boyfriend loaned me his car. I eventually bought myself another car. With this new small amount of freedom came a small price to pay. My ex-boyfriend would follow me around and hide down the road watching me at my new boyfriend's house in the country. I knew he was there because I every so often caught him hiding.

One day I was at my new boyfriend's house and my sister-in-law called me and told me my ex-boyfriend wanted to talk to me. She told me to be careful and not to go by myself. I went to his house. I had my four children with me. I made the children stay in the car while I talked to him. He begged me to come back to him. I told him I had moved on. I went to leave and he wouldn't move away from the door. I was scared. He pulled out a gun he had behind the door. Some how while he was getting the gun, I got the courage to run out the door. I ran and jumped in the car and sped out the dirt lane like crazy. I could not go to my apartment, and I could not go back to my boyfriend's house because no one was home. I went to my sister-in law's home. The four children and I hurried into her house. Shortly there after he pulled up and knocked on her door. I was even more scared. She answered the door. He wanted to talk to me. I was afraid to for my safety, and everybody's safety that was with me.

I stood back from the door. He said, "I won't hurt you." I told him again that I moved on and I was not interested in coming back to him. He then talked a little to my sister in law. He eventually left with no further problems. In hind site I should have called the police, but I was afraid. God saved my children and me from my unhealthy decisions and myself again. My children and I stayed the night with my new boyfriend at his home because I was afraid my ex-boyfriend would come to my apartment when I was home alone. I also felt more secure with my new boyfriend because he was an ex-policeman.

Chapter 14
The New Family

My new boy friend had three children from his previous marriage. His ex wife let him have the children. I had four children from my previous marriage. Together we had seven children. We started dating more and my children and I started spending more time at his home. He was a racecar driver at a local dirt track. My children and his children and I would go together and watch him race. All nine of us got along fine. After about a year of dating, my boyfriend asked me to move in with my children. My children and I agreed to move in with him and his three children. Things were good at first. Then I realized he had no rules for his children. I am a rule person. Growing up with so many rules really influenced me. I became the mean stepmother to his children. His children started giving me a hard time.

One day my ex-husband and his new wife refused to return my son after visitations. I called the police about the problem. They told me to meet them at my ex-husbands apartment, and that we would all go from there. The police went in and returned my son to me after a short ordeal. My ex-husband was always trying to turn my children against me. He would tell them terrible lies about me, and make everything I did seem like it was bad.

I started to take notice that my boyfriend was drinking beer everyday. He started going out more often to the bars. I tried to talk to him. I told him we needed counseling if he wanted me to stay. I was still taking my son to the hospital for check ups for his leukemia and one day I just opened up to my son's social worker. The social worker suggested we seek counseling closer to home. The social worker gave me a name and number to contact. I contacted this counselor as soon as I could.

We started with family counseling. We then changed to couples counseling after several family sessions. He stopped going to counseling but I kept going. This was the second best thing I could do for my children and myself. My counselor stated to me one day that for some unknown reason that I wanted out of the dysfunctional life. The unknown reason was God, but I hadn't realized that yet. I later in life discovered this. The counseling was my first step God had for me in breaking the dysfunctional cycle. My boyfriend started coming home very drunk. He was not ugly when he was drunk but the fact that he came home like that in front of the children was unbearable.

I started to see things differently through counseling. God was opening my eyes. I realized I had an addiction problem to men who were emotionally unavailable. I am a woman who loves too much. I realized I was an enabler. I realized my boyfriend was a functional alcoholic and that he refused to change. I had finally had enough with his alcoholism. I moved to an apartment with my four children, and continued to go to counseling. I joined a women's group for support.

I realized I came from a very dysfunctional family. I realized no one ever told me, "I love you," as I was growing up. No one ever hugged me, or did anything to show affection. I remember my grandmother always telling me, "You're lucky your mom doesn't put you and your brothers and sister in a home for children." She frequently told me things like that. My grandmother often told me she hated blondes and would say, "Look what I got for a granddaughter." I had that wretched blonde hair. Then I had a mother and father in name only. I realized that there were a lot of alcoholic's in my childhood and I grew to think that it was normal, or that it wasn't out of the ordinary. I realized I was a lost person out there, trying to raise four children by myself. I realized I blamed everyone else for my problems. I realized I was always yelling at my children, like I was always yelled at when I was growing up. I realized I did not tell my children that I loved them, like I was not told while I was growing up. I realized that I was hitting my children on the hands all the time for reasons they shouldn't have been. I learned that I was talking for my children. I learned that I carried on the cycle with my children and taught them dysfunctional behavior. I learned that I was not saying things in the proper way. I had to teach myself how to speak without putting the other person on the defense.

I realized a woman who loves too much has a partner who is inappropriate, uncaring, or unavailable and cannot give him up easily or at all. In fact they want him and they need him even more. Their loving itself becomes an addiction. Women who love too much are addicted to pain and suffering. I learned that one addiction feeds another and that is why I chose the men I chose. I learned that my childhood experiences and dynamics caused the obsession with relationships and the cycle. I realized I came from a dysfunctional home where my emotional needs were not met. I realized I had no real nurturing. In an attempt to fill my unmet needs I chose men who had an addiction and were needy. I realized I was in a pattern where I tried to be the loving caretaker and would try to change my man through my love. I realized you cannot change someone for the better if you are not well yourself.

I realized I was afraid of abandonment. So I would abandon the relationship first. I was accustomed to a lack of love, so I would try harder to please. I realized I had a very low self-esteem and I had a desperate need to control my men. I realized I was not attracted to men who are kind, stable, reliable, and interested in me. I found nice men boring.

During counseling I learned I had a mild OCD behavior. OCD is an anxiety disorder characterized by obsessions and compulsions. Some people only experience one or the other. Compulsions are repetitive behaviors that attempt to neutralize existing feelings of anxiety. I had the habit of checking things repeatedly. I made sure the doors were locked before leaving the house by repeatedly checking the lock. I would also check the windows repeatedly to make sure they were locked before leaving the house. Also I would check candles repeatedly to make sure I blew it out before I would leave the house. The stovetops were repeatedly checked to make sure I turned the burners off before leaving the house. The OCD habit of checking things too much is associated with the need to have safety and security and the obsession of avoiding harm and danger. I would dust everyday because I had the fear that my house was dirty and someone would take my children away from me. Through counseling and dealing with my other addictions in my life and with Gods help my OCD has lessened greatly. This is why my sister's messiness drove me crazy. My children later in life made me aware that I drove them crazy with my constant cleaning and having things organized and reorganized. I learned through counseling that I am okay if I have some dust on the furniture or if something is slightly out of place. I had to talk to myself daily and reprogram myself.

I continued in counseling for a couple of years. I changed my behaviors and the way I related to my children and others. This change was very hard. I had to teach myself not to yell and hit my children's hands. I had to think everyday about what I was saying and doing. I had to learn to think positive and say positive things. I had to learn to keep my head up and stop looking at the ground. I had to learn how to express my emotions in a proper way and I had to learn how to listen to my inner child and learn how to love her.

I always hated if someone was talking to me and touched me. I would cringe inside. I had to teach myself to hug myself and other people. I freely give hugs now. I had to teach myself how to love myself. I had to learn how to stop blaming others for my problems and take responsibility for them myself. This process took years, a lot of tears and talking to myself. I had to go back to my childhood and deal with all the hurt and things that happened to me. At the time I was not aware that God was by my side and that he was guiding me in the right direction.

My ex-boyfriend started to go to counseling for himself. He started to go to AA meetings. He started to call me and talk to me differently. He started to write me letters all the time. I had my guard up though. It took me a long time to let my guard down for him. Eventually we started dating again. Things were different this time.

About a year or so later my four children and I moved back with him in his home. We became engaged, and we lived together for about ten years before we got married. We both had children in college and tuition is less expensive if you are a single parent. His youngest daughter went to live with her mother because she did not like the rules I set. She was his only child at home anymore.

We got married in a church where my husband had attended before. I liked the pastor. We started attending this church. I had a hard time dealing with going to church. In the back of my mind I would hear my mother saying, "Witnesses do not go into other churches." I spoke with my counselor who helped me deal with my mother's voice in the back of my head.

My oldest daughter became pregnant in her senior year and gave me my first grandson. I was getting prepared to start to work full time due to all the children being in high school or out of school. I promised my daughter I would continue to work part time and baby-sat my grandson on my days off. She now is a bank teller at a local bank.

My second oldest daughter became pregnant in her senior year too and gave me my first granddaughter. She went on to a nearby college and is now a schoolteacher. Today I have a total of three grandsons and two granddaughters.

Chapter 15
Discovering God

The pastor of the church retired. We felt lost and did not feel comfortable with the next pastor. We stopped attending church. I had a nagging voice in the back of my head saying, "You need to go to church." God was speaking to me. One day at work we had a new woman doctor making rounds. She was very nice. As time passed I came to know she was very religious. One day she invited me to an Alpha Course. I was afraid to attend the course because I thought the people would be pushy. I discussed it with my husband and he agreed to go with me to the Alpha Course. My husband told me, "I'm only doing this for you."

I was still afraid and had reservations. As we started the course I was still afraid they would be pushy. They were not pushy at all. We attended the entire Alpha Course. I absolutely loved it. They actually enlightened me. This was the best thing God had in store for me. I attended a second Alpha Course with my oldest daughter.

I discovered through Alpha that God was with me all my life, and pushing me to do better for myself, and was saving me from myself and my bad decisions I made in my life. Before Alpha, I did not want to hear about God or Jesus due to my strict religious childhood. I did not pray. I avoided anything or any situation regarding God. I seldom attended church. I was a lost soul. What happened to me at Alpha turned me around in a positive way.

Alpha gave me the beginnings of understanding what a Christian means. It gave me warm Christian friendship with a sense of belonging. It put me on firm ground to travel on my journey with God. In my life after Alpha I am hungry for God and Jesus. I attend church as often as possible. I pray everyday. I now talk to others about God very often. I now take vacation days from work on Sundays so I can attend church. I send religious related messages to people I care about. I have asked Jesus to please come into my life by his Holy Spirit, and to be with me forever.

God is my heavenly father who guides me and listens to me whenever and wherever I talk to him. I get on my knees and thank God for taking me out of my very dysfunctional life and putting me in this new life and church. I thank God; he gave me the wisdom, courage, and strength to change my life and to lead me to the church where I am. I now have God's knowledge and wisdom to help my children and grandchildren.

Through God I am now a better person, wife, mother, grandmother, friend and nurse. My husband now attends church with and without me. We also attend Sunday school. I attend women's Bible study. My husband attends men's Bible study. I have learned that God promises to guide me. I have learned that God has a good plan for my life and that all that has happened to me was part of his plan.

I feel like I did a terrible injustice to my children by not taking them to church and teaching them about God. I wish God had taken me out of the dysfunctional life sooner so that I would not have taught my children the dysfunctional cycle. I know God did what he did as part of his plan. So I can only sit back and let him run his course.

Chapter 16
My family

My oldest daughter has two sons and is a single mother. She has a job as a bank teller. My second daughter is married and has two daughters and is a schoolteacher. My son is married and has no children. He is a cancer survivor and is going strong. All the children who were diagnosed when he was diagnosed have all passed away. God kept my son on this earth for a reason. My son and his wife are trying to have children. The doctors think my son has abnormal sperm due to the chemotherapy he had when he was little. He is a computer tech for a local school district. My youngest daughter is married and has a son. She works at an ice cream store decorating cakes and as a nurse's aid. She is also taking college courses via the Internet. She plans to be an English teacher.

I am the grandmother to my grandchildren that my mother never was to my children. I have baby-sat all my grandchildren since birth. I was there for the first day of school for all of my grandchildren. I would call off sick to stay home with my sick grandchildren. I would take my grandchildren to the dentist and doctor. I also took them to the emergency room at the hospital when needed. We have taken my grandchildren to the beach and Disney

World on vacation with us. I have loved and nurtured my grandchildren. They thrive on my love, hugs, kisses and positive words, which are only possible since God took me out of my dysfunctional life.

I have been through some hard times with choices my children have made through the dysfunctional cycle. My youngest daughter got herself into an abusive and drug addicted relationship with a man who lived with her and her baby son. He is not the father of my grandson. Her boyfriend did not like my grandson who was six months old. My grandson cried when the boyfriend was alone with him. One day my daughter dropped off my grandson for me to baby sit. He was sleepy so I laid on the waterbed with him to sleep. He did not roll over like he usually did. When he woke up I picked him up and changed his diaper. I then proceeded to dress him. His right arm was limp and he cried when I moved it. I called my daughter at work and told her something was wrong with her son.

My daughter, her boyfriend, and I took him to the doctor who sent us to the hospital for x-rays. The x-ray showed he had a fractured arm. The hospital called the doctor who ordered a full body cat scan. The scan showed my grandson had five fractured bones, the right collarbone, the right upper arm, both wrists, and an old fracture in his left lower leg. I was furious. The doctor and the hospital called children and youth for child abuse. My grandson was only six months old. I cried for him. He was hospitalized for a few days for his own safety. Children and Youth took my grandson from my daughter and gave me temporary custody. My grandson had to have a cast on his right arm. The police and Children and Youth questioned my daughter and her boyfriend. My daughter was innocent. Her boyfriend was charged with child abuse and several other charges. He was denying the charges. We had to prepare to go to court for the child abuse case. He later changed his mind and pleaded guilty for lesser time in jail. My daughter's boyfriend got my grandson out of his crib that morning and abused him causing the fractures. This ex-boyfriend was sent to the state prison for child abuse.

I am now dealing with my oldest grandson and his addiction to alcohol and marijuana. I saw what was happening and made my daughter aware. My daughter was in denial. My grandson started getting in trouble at school and with the law. He was treating the family very different. He started lying, stealing from his family, and coming home drunk or high. Things were getting worse. He was placed in out of school suspension. He was placed on house arrest for hot urine. After house arrest he had another hot urine while on probation. The probation officer told him he could go before the judge and end up in a juvenile detention center or he could go to rehab for six months. My grandson chose rehab. I was there when he was taken away to rehab. I cried and prayed for him. He is currently still in rehab. He is doing well in rehab. He has learned about God in rehab. We write letters back and forth to each other. I visit him when we are allowed to. I keep on praying for him that God will help him like he helped me out of Satan's chains.

My husband, my oldest daughter, and my two youngest grandsons all attend church. My oldest granddaughter occasionally attends church with us. I have taken my youngest grandson and granddaughter to vacation Bible school this past summer. I hope to open their eyes and let them see that God is good.

I thank God for helping me break the chains of Satan's that were holding me in bondage. I am still learning to live in the freedom God has given me. I know Satan waits for opportunities when we are vulnerable and he likes keeping you held down. God' s good from life's bad is one of the most liberating concepts in the entire Word of God. God has promised well out of anything we encounter as long as we love him and allow him to use it for his purpose.

I have learned to trust God to help me in difficult times. I know that God does not minimize things that break our hearts. God wants us to grow through our hurts. God does not want us to ignore our hurts. God wants us to draw closer to him in times of heartache. Only God can put the pieces of our hearts back together again. This is what God has done for me in my life.

Satan was the author of my dysfunctional and abusive childhood story. The Bible is the strongest bandage God uses to mend hearts broken in childhood.

God knows how badly I wanted to be free from the power of abuse and dysfunctional cycles. God wants us to come to him not timidly, anxious, or out of fear of how he might respond to us. God wants to help us. God has all the grace we need to confront any challenge if we go to him.

Satan's lies, keep us walking in our chains. I pray that God will continue to help me avoid snares and pitfalls in my earthly journey. I pray that God will continue to fill my empty spaces with his unfailing love. The more I learn God's word the quicker I recognize Satan's attempts to place me back into his chains. I have learned to reprogram myself out of captivity through the truth. The truth shall make me free.

God's word is the truth. I have learned how to overcome, but I still remember what it was like to be broken. Love God with all your heart. Awareness is the first step to freedom. I thank God he was strong in my weakness. God, I pray that I am a display of your splendor. God is awesome to have saved a wretch like me.

CPSIA information can be obtained at www.ICGtesting.com
Printed in the USA
BVOW011905220312

285861BV00001B/10/P